My First Riddle

The South West

Edited By Machaela Gavaghan

First published in Great Britain in 2019 by:

Young Writers Est. 1991

Young Writers
Remus House
Coltsfoot Drive
Peterborough
PE2 9BF
Telephone: 01733 890066
Website: www.youngwriters.co.uk

All Rights Reserved
Book Design by Ashley Janson
© Copyright Contributors 2019
Softback ISBN 978-1-78988-755-6
Hardback ISBN 978-1-83928-131-0
Printed and bound in the UK by BookPrintingUK
Website: www.bookprintinguk.com
YB0414V

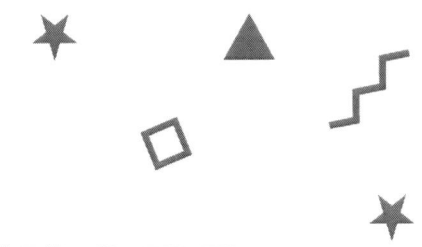

FOREWORD

Dear Reader,

Are you ready to get your thinking caps on to puzzle your way through this wonderful collection?

Young Writers are proud to introduce our new poetry competition, *My First Riddle*, designed to introduce Reception pupils to the delights of poetry. Riddles are a great way to introduce children to the use of poetic expression, including description, similes and expanded noun phrases, as well as encouraging them to 'think outside the box' by providing clues without giving the answer away immediately. Some pupils were given a series of riddle templates to choose from, giving them a framework within which to shape their ideas.

Their answers could be whatever or whoever their imaginations desired; from people to places, animals to objects, food to seasons. All of us here at Young Writers believe in the importance of inspiring young children to produce creative writing, including poetry, and we feel that seeing their own riddles in print will ignite that spark of creativity.

We hope you enjoy riddling your way through this book as much as we enjoyed reading all the entries.

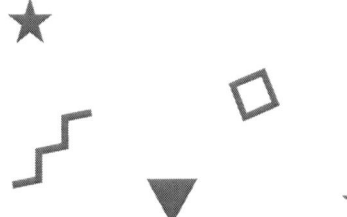

CONTENTS

Avondale School, Bulford

Declan Joseph Gibbs (5)	1
Vhukhudo Mudau (5)	2
Hudson Ovenden (5)	3
Grace Isabella Margaret Ehlen (5)	4
Jasper Forster (4)	5

Carmel Christian School, Brislington

Hannah Carson (5)	6
Elishah Leo (5)	7
Shiloh Woodford (5)	8

Ellwood Community Primary School, Ellwood

Zachariah Michael Gilchrist-Winman (5)	9
Aimie Roberts (5)	10
Macey-Rose Field (4)	11
Ruby Aston (4)	12
Brady May (5)	13
Darcie Olivia Rose Teague (4)	14
Cecelia Ruth Cornish (5)	15
Oscar Edge (4)	16

Emersons Green Primary School, Emersons Green

Toby Birtles (5)	17
Esmae Lillianna Thorne (4)	18
Olivia Cheasley (5)	19
Grace Bennett (5)	20
Leo Ricco (5)	21

Dilraj Singh (4)	22

Frogwell Primary School, Chippenham

Edward Widger (5)	23
Ismay White (4)	24
Emily Jefferies (5)	25
Lewis Courtney-West (5)	26
Lilly-May Palmer (5)	27
Jacob Bain (5)	28
Christian Greenwell (5)	29
Arabella Jayne Lintern (4)	30
Alfie Jefferies (5)	31
Olivia Rose Billett (4)	32
Lilly Detain (5)	33

Hatherleigh Community Primary School, Okehampton

Eva-Rose Greensill (5)	34
Charlie Rotheray (5)	35
Louie Friggens (5)	36
Jack Bowyer (5)	37
Daisy Packham (5)	38
Lillie Duncan (5)	39

Oakwood Primary School, Cheltenham

Jasmine May Lane (5)	40

Ruishton Primary Academy, Ruishton

Freddie Hill (5)	41
Soffera Nevill (5)	42

Millie Patricia Anne Giles (5)	43
Paddy Philpots	44
Ewan Loveridge (5)	45
Sylvie Hopkins (5)	46
Jacob May (5)	47
James Joyce (5)	48
Georgie Scribbins (5)	49
Lois Scribbins (5)	50

St Michael's CE Primary School, Stoke Gifford

Niall Hackett (5)	51
Kian McMillan (5)	52
Omisha Gulla (5)	53
Nicole Celma (4)	54
Vihaan Arun (4)	55
Nicol Abbas (5)	56
Hannah Downie (5)	57
Jessica Lewis (5)	58
Rohan Mehta (5)	59
Aila Geddes (5)	60
Connor Wotton (4)	61
Lyla Viney (4)	62

St Paul's CE Primary School, Gloucester

Tom Sinoradzki (5)	63
Ricards Savickis (4)	64
Calvin Omari Francis (4)	65

Stalbridge CE Primary School, Stalbridge

Esther Bennett (4)	66
Leo Fortino (4)	67
Oliver Newberry (5)	68
Aurelia Lux Turner (5)	69
Edward Mitchell (5)	70
Harry Stickland (5)	71
Nathan Collins (5)	72
Marley Beau Cooper (5)	73

Treleigh Community Primary School, Treleigh

Tabitha Emily Williams (5)	74
Dottie Ellen Valentine Till (5)	75
Aiden Hill (5)	76
Lottie Maybank (5)	77
Tiberius Moore (5)	78
Emilia Woodard (4)	79
Abbie Williams	80
Orla Bray (5)	81
Thomas Peerless (5)	82
Dylan Merrett-Cope (4)	83
Ezmae Cooke (5)	84
Jowan Kershaw (4)	85
Sapphire Mitchell (5)	86
Erin Millard (5)	87
Lewis Pooley (5)	88

Trewirgie Infants' School, Redruth

Max Sims (4)	89
Laura Stukaite (5)	90
Clara Davies (5)	91
Ollie Jack Hutchens (5)	92
Olivia Cooper (5)	93
Phoenix (5) & Alanna	94
Noah Jones (5)	95
Violet Mckenzie (5)	96
Alia Marie Blaber (4)	97
Alfie Thomas Hart (4)	98
Amelia Natasha Hunter (5)	99
Harvey Imchichi (5)	100
Jessica Lowndes (5)	101
Cody Holloway (5)	102
Sophie Miller (5)	103
Isla Clarke (5)	104
Harlan Massey (5)	105
Alex Guppy-Wilcox (5)	106
James Pullin (5)	107
Mason Summers (5)	108
Isla Roberts (5)	109
Millie Smith (4)	110

Lando Winchester (5), Lennon, Gabriella Wooten, Harley, Lily-Lea (5), Elsa Victoria-Louise Hill & Kennedy Mila Allison	111
Laith Wills (4)	112
Summer Crocker (4), Ethan, Laylah & Archie Jacka	113
Florie Creeden (4)	114
Lola Curnow (5)	115
Luke Matthews (5)	116
Alanna Freya Isaacs (5)	117
Elian Thomas (4)	118
Arya Spry (5)	119
Cohen Taylor (5)	120
Mollie Jonik (5)	121

Wareham St Mary Primary School, Wareham

Dylan Finley Robert King (5)	122
Harlie Fenton (5)	123
Emilija Hughes (4)	124
Keira-Leigh Baynton (5)	125
Rory McConnell (5)	126
Zachary Lee Knowles (5)	127
Molly Lee (5)	128
Alexandra Pitman (5)	129
Peter John Nurdin (5)	130
Sienna Helen Wells (5)	131
Emily Chrissy Williams (5)	132
Jacob Hobbs-Smith (5)	133

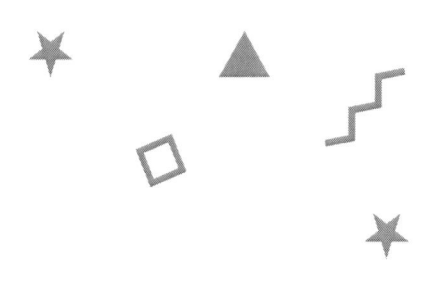

THE RIDDLES

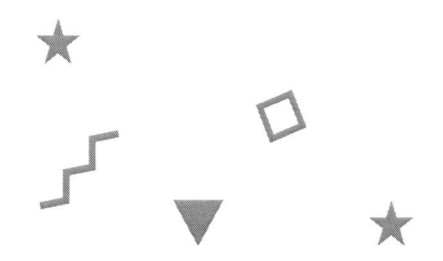

Declan's First Riddle

What could it be?
Follow the clues and see.

It looks **metallic**.
It sounds like *bleep, bloop!*
It smells like **lightning**.
It feels **strong and tough**.
It tastes like **machinery**.

Have you guessed what it could be?
Look below and you will see,
It is...

Answer: A robot.

Declan Joseph Gibbs (5)
Avondale School, Bulford

Vhukhudo's First Riddle

What could she be?
Follow the clues and see.

She looks **beautiful**.
She sounds like **birds singing**.
She smells like **lovely roses**.
She feels **really smooth**.
She tastes **yucky**.

Have you guessed what she could be?
Look below and you will see,
She is...

Answer: A princess.

Vhukhudo Mudau (5)
Avondale School, Bulford

Hudson's First Riddle

What could it be?
Follow the clues and see.

It looks **fun**.
It sounds like **whoosh**!
It smells like **rubber**.
It feels **fast and smooth**.
It tastes **cold**.

Have you guessed what it could be?
Look below and you will see,
It is...

Answer: A scooter.

Hudson Ovenden (5)
Avondale School, Bulford

Grace's First Riddle

What could it be?
Follow the clues and see.

It looks like **the moon**.
It sounds like **sizzling in a pan**.
It smells **yummy**.
It feels **soft**.
It tastes **great with lemon and sugar**.

Have you guessed what it could be?
Look below and you will see,
It is...

Answer: A pancake.

Grace Isabella Margaret Ehlen (5)
Avondale School, Bulford

Jasper's First Riddle

What could it be?
Follow the clues and see.

It looks **bouncy**.
It sounds **fun**.
It smells like **fresh air**.
It feels **springy**.
It tastes like **grass**.

Have you guessed what it could be?
Look below and you will see,
It is...

Answer: *A trampoline.*

Jasper Forster (4)
Avondale School, Bulford

Hannah's First Riddle

What could it be?
Follow the clues and see.

It looks like **a traffic light**.
It sounds like **nothing**.
It smells **sweet**.
It feels **spongy**.
It tastes like **fruit**.

Have you guessed what it could be?
Look below and you will see,
It is...

Answer: A mango.

Hannah Carson (5)
Carmel Christian School, Brislington

My First Riddle - The South West

Elishah's First Riddle

What could it be?
Follow the clues and see.

It looks **green and red**.
It sounds **crunchy**.
It smells like **leaves**.
It feels **soft**.
It tastes **sharp**.

Have you guessed what it could be?
Look below and you will see,
It is...

Answer: Rhubarb.

Elishah Leo (5)
Carmel Christian School, Brislington

Shiloh's First Riddle

What could it be?
Follow the clues and see.

It looks **green**.
It sounds **crunchy**.
It smells **strong**.
It feels **squishy**.
It tastes **crunchy**.

Have you guessed what it could be?
Look below and you will see,
It is...

Answer: Broccoli.

Shiloh Woodford (5)
Carmel Christian School, Brislington

Zachariah's First Riddle

What could it be?
Follow the clues and see.

It looks **white**.
It sounds like ***cluck, cluck***!
It smells **delicious**.
It feels **fluffy**.
It tastes **yummy**.

Have you guessed what it could be?
Look below and you will see,
It is...

Answer: A cooked chicken.

Zachariah Michael Gilchrist-Winman (5)
Ellwood Community Primary School, Ellwood

Aimie's First Riddle

What could it be?
Follow the clues and see.

It looks **green and yellow**.
It sounds like **a drum**.
It smells **juicy**.
It feels **hard**.
It tastes **fruity**.

Have you guessed what it could be?
Look below and you will see,
It is...

Answer: A watermelon.

Aimie Roberts (5)
Ellwood Community Primary School, Ellwood

My First Riddle - The South West

Macey-Rose's First Riddle

What could it be?
Follow the clues and see.

It looks **brown**.
It sounds **crunchy**.
It smells **yummy**.
It feels **smooth**.
It tastes **creamy and yummy**.

Have you guessed what it could be?
Look below and you will see,
It is...

Answer: Chocolate.

Macey-Rose Field (4)
Ellwood Community Primary School, Ellwood

Ruby's First Riddle

What could it be?
Follow the clues and see.

It looks **yellow**.
It sounds **crunchy**.
It smells **yummy**.
It feels **hard**.
It tastes **nice**.

Have you guessed what it could be?
Look below and you will see,
It is...

Answer: A chicken.

Ruby Aston (4)
Ellwood Community Primary School, Ellwood

Brady's First Riddle

What could it be?
Follow the clues and see.

It looks **round**.
It sounds **crunchy**.
It smells **tasty**.
It feels **soft**.
It tastes **yummy**.

Have you guessed what it could be?
Look below and you will see,
It is...

Answer: An apple.

Brady May (5)
Ellwood Community Primary School, Ellwood

Darcie's First Riddle

What could it be?
Follow the clues and see.

It looks **blue**.
It sounds **drippy**.
It smells **fresh**.
It feels **wet**.
It tastes like **water**.

Have you guessed what it could be?
Look below and you will see,
It is...

Answer: Rain.

Darcie Olivia Rose Teague (4)
Ellwood Community Primary School, Ellwood

Cecelia's First Riddle

What could it be?
Follow the clues and see.

It looks **tall**.
It sounds **crunchy**.
It smells **yummy**.
It feels **cold**.
It tastes **sweet**.

Have you guessed what it could be?
Look below and you will see,
It is...

Answer: A lolly.

Cecelia Ruth Cornish (5)
Ellwood Community Primary School, Ellwood

Oscar's First Riddle

What could it be?
Follow the clues and see.

It looks **furry**.
It sounds **loud**.
It smells **dirty**.
It feels **nice**.
It tastes **yucky**.

Have you guessed what it could be?
Look below and you will see,
It is...

Answer: A lion.

Oscar Edge (4)
Ellwood Community Primary School, Ellwood

… My First Riddle - The South West

Toby's First Riddle

What could it be?
Follow the clues and see.

It looks like **fairy sparkles**.
It sounds like **fairy magic**.
It smells like **fairy strawberries**.
It feels like **a warm kiss and cuddle**.
It tastes like **fairy dust**.

Have you guessed what it could be?
Look below and you will see,
It is…

Answer: A rainbow.

Toby Birtles (5)
Emersons Green Primary School, Emersons Green

Esmae's First Riddle

What could it be?
Follow the clues and see.

It looks **white and fluffy**.
It sounds like **a wolf**.
It smells like **fur and mud**.
It feels **soft and cuddly with a wet nose**.
It tastes **yucky and hairy**!

Have you guessed what it could be?
Look below and you will see,
It is...

Answer: My golden retriever, Skye.

Esmae Lillianna Thorne (4)
Emersons Green Primary School, Emersons Green

Olivia's First Riddle

What could it be?
Follow the clues and see.

It looks **purple**.
It sounds **splashy**.
It smells **sweet**.
It feels **smooth**.
It tastes like **apple and blackcurrant**.

Have you guessed what it could be?
Look below and you will see,
It is...

Answer: A Fruit Shoot.

Olivia Cheasley (5)
Emersons Green Primary School, Emersons Green

Grace's First Riddle

What could it be?
Follow the clues and see.

It looks like **the sun**.
It sounds **squirty**.
It smells **fresh**.
It feels **soft**.
It tastes **bitter**.

Have you guessed what it could be?
Look below and you will see,
It is…

Answer: A lemon.

Grace Bennett (5)
Emersons Green Primary School, Emersons Green

Leo's First Riddle

What could it be?
Follow the clues and see.

It looks **shiny**.
It sounds **crunchy**.
It smells **sweet**.
It feels **smooth**.
It tastes **yummy**.

Have you guessed what it could be?
Look below and you will see,
It is...

Answer: An apple.

Leo Ricco (5)
Emersons Green Primary School, Emersons Green

Dilraj's First Riddle

What could it be?
Follow the clues and see.

It looks **cheesy**.
It sounds **sizzly**.
It smells **Italian**.
It feels **soft**.
It tastes **crispy**.

Have you guessed what it could be?
Look below and you will see,
It is...

Answer: A pizza.

Dilraj Singh (4)
Emersons Green Primary School, Emersons Green

Edward's First Riddle

What could it be?
Follow the clues and see.

It looks **stripy**.
It sounds **quiet and scary**.
It smells like **grass**.
It feels **soft and dangerous**.
It tastes **scratchy like oranges**.

Have you guessed what it could be?
Look below and you will see,
It is...

Answer: A tiger.

Edward Widger (5)
Frogwell Primary School, Chippenham

Ismay's First Riddle

What could it be?
Follow the clues and see.

It looks **white and sparkly**.
It sounds like **a horse**.
It smells like **a rainbow**.
It feels like **silk**.
It tastes like **candyfloss**.

Have you guessed what it could be?
Look below and you will see,
It is...

Answer: A unicorn.

Ismay White (4)
Frogwell Primary School, Chippenham

Emily's First Riddle

What could it be?
Follow the clues and see.

It looks like **it has clothes on**.
It **has no sound**.
It smells **old and dirty**.
It feels like **a statue**.
It tastes like **straw**.

Have you guessed what it could be?
Look below and you will see,
It is...

Answer: A scarecrow.

Emily Jefferies (5)
Frogwell Primary School, Chippenham

Lewis' First Riddle

What could it be?
Follow the clues and see.

It looks like **a falling star**.
It sounds **quiet**.
It smells like **Christmas**.
It feels **cold**.
It tastes **crunchy and icy**.

Have you guessed what it could be?
Look below and you will see,
It is...

Answer: A snowflake.

Lewis Courtney-West (5)
Frogwell Primary School, Chippenham

Lilly-May's First Riddle

What could it be?
Follow the clues and see.

It looks **colourful**.
It sounds like **a horse**.
It smells like **candyfloss**.
It feels **silky and soft**.
It tastes like **Skittles**.

Have you guessed what it could be?
Look below and you will see,
It is...

Answer: A unicorn.

Lilly-May Palmer (5)
Frogwell Primary School, Chippenham

Jacob's First Riddle

What could it be?
Follow the clues and see.

It looks **green and scary**.
It sounds **loud and roary**.
It smells **muddy**.
It feels **hard and spiky**.
It tastes like **meat**.

Have you guessed what it could be?
Look below and you will see,
It is...

Answer: A dinosaur.

Jacob Bain (5)
Frogwell Primary School, Chippenham

My First Riddle - The South West

Christian's First Riddle

What could it be?
Follow the clues and see.

It looks **colourful**.
It sounds like **'power'**.
It smells **beautiful**.
It feels **soft**.
It tastes like **a garden**.

Have you guessed what it could be?
Look below and you will see,
It is...

Answer: *A flower.*

Christian Greenwell (5)
Frogwell Primary School, Chippenham

Arabella's First Riddle

What could it be?
Follow the clues and see.

It looks **brown with a red chest**.
It sounds **happy**.
It smells like **seeds**.
It feels **soft**.
It **likes worms and bread**.

Have you guessed what it could be?
Look below and you will see,
It is...

Answer: A robin.

Arabella Jayne Lintern (4)
Frogwell Primary School, Chippenham

My First Riddle - The South West

Alfie's First Riddle

What could it be?
Follow the clues and see.

It looks **lovely**.
It sounds like **waves**.
It smells like **the sea**.
It feels **wet and sandy**.
It tastes like **salt**.

Have you guessed what it could be?
Look below and you will see,
It is...

Answer: *The beach.*

Alfie Jefferies (5)
Frogwell Primary School, Chippenham

Olivia's First Riddle

What could it be?
Follow the clues and see.

It looks **green and speckled**.
It sounds **croaky**.
It smells like **a pond**.
It feels **slimy**.
It **eats flies**.

Have you guessed what it could be?
Look below and you will see,
It is...

Answer: A frog.

Olivia Rose Billett (4)
Frogwell Primary School, Chippenham

Lilly's First Riddle

What could it be?
Follow the clues and see.

It looks **pretty**.
It sounds **quiet**.
It smells **lovely**.
It feels **soft**.
It tastes **horrible**.

Have you guessed what it could be?
Look below and you will see,
It is...

Answer: A flower.

Lilly Detain (5)
Frogwell Primary School, Chippenham

Eva-Rose's First Riddle

What could it be?
Follow the clues and see.

It looks **beautiful**.
It sounds **quiet**.
It smells like **fruit**.
It feels **delicate**.
It tastes like **candyfloss**.

Have you guessed what it could be?
Look below and you will see,
It is...

Answer: A **butterfly**.

Eva-Rose Greensill (5)
Hatherleigh Community Primary School, Okehampton

Charlie's First Riddle

What could it be?
Follow the clues and see.

It looks **orange and black**.
It sounds like **roaring**.
It smells **stinky**.
It feels **soft**.
It tastes like **meat**.

Have you guessed what it could be?
Look below and you will see,
It is...

Answer: A *tiger*.

Charlie Rotheray (5)
Hatherleigh Community Primary School, Okehampton

Louie's First Riddle

What could it be?
Follow the clues and see.

It looks **grey**.
It sounds like **a trumpet**.
It smells **stinky**.
It feels **rough**.
It tastes like **peanuts**.

Have you guessed what it could be?
Look below and you will see,
It is...

Answer: An elephant.

Louie Friggens (5)
Hatherleigh Community Primary School, Okehampton

Jack's First Riddle

What could it be?
Follow the clues and see.

It looks **black and orange**.
It sounds **fierce**.
It smells **stinky**.
It feels **soft**.
It tastes like **meat**.

Have you guessed what it could be?
Look below and you will see,
It is...

Answer: A tiger.

Jack Bowyer (5)
Hatherleigh Community Primary School, Okehampton

Daisy's First Riddle

What could it be?
Follow the clues and see.

It looks **round**.
It sounds **crunchy**.
It smells **nice and sweet**.
It feels **smooth**.
It tastes **nice**.

Have you guessed what it could be?
Look below and you will see,
It is...

Answer: An apple.

Daisy Packham (5)
Hatherleigh Community Primary School, Okehampton

Lillie's First Riddle

What could it be?
Follow the clues and see.

It looks **lovely**.
It sounds **quiet**.
It smells like **flowers**.
It feels **soft**.
It tastes **sweet**.

Have you guessed what it could be?
Look below and you will see,
It is...

Answer: A **butterfly**.

Lillie Duncan (5)
Hatherleigh Community Primary School, Okehampton

Jasmine's First Riddle

What could it be?
Follow the clues and see.

It looks **bumpy**.
It sounds like **the ocean**.
It smells **fishy**.
It feels **smooth**.
It tastes **salty**.

Have you guessed what it could be?
Look below and you will see,
It is...

Answer: A shell.

Jasmine May Lane (5)
Oakwood Primary School, Cheltenham

Freddie's First Riddle

What could it be?
Follow the clues and see.

It looks **black and white and round**.
It sounds like *thud, thud!*
It smells like **cut grass**.
It feels **hard and smooth**.
It tastes like **leather**.

Have you guessed what it could be?
Look below and you will see,
It is...

Answer: A football.

Freddie Hill (5)
Ruishton Primary Academy, Ruishton

Soffera's First Riddle

What could it be?
Follow the clues and see.

It looks like **a ball**.
It sounds **hollow**.
It smells **sweet**.
It feels **hard outside and soft inside**.
It tastes **yummy**.

Have you guessed what it could be?
Look below and you will see,
It is...

Answer: A watermelon.

Soffera Nevill (5)
Ruishton Primary Academy, Ruishton

My First Riddle - The South West

Millie's First Riddle

What could it be?
Follow the clues and see.

It looks like **a love heart**.
It sounds like **a berry**.
It smells **as sweet as candy**.
It feels **prickly**.
It tastes **yummy with cream**.

Have you guessed what it could be?
Look below and you will see,
It is...

Answer: A strawberry.

Millie Patricia Anne Giles (5)
Ruishton Primary Academy, Ruishton

Paddy's First Riddle

What could it be?
Follow the clues and see.

It looks **round**.
It sounds like **a thud**.
It smells like **leather and grass**.
It feels **hard and smooth**.
It tastes like **eating rubber**.

Have you guessed what it could be?
Look below and you will see,
It is...

Answer: *A football.*

Paddy Philpots
Ruishton Primary Academy, Ruishton

Ewan's First Riddle

What could it be?
Follow the clues and see.

It looks **round**.
It sounds like *boing*.
It smells like **rubber**.
It feels **smooth**.
It tastes **disgusting**!

Have you guessed what it could be?
Look below and you will see,
It is...

Answer: A ball.

Ewan Loveridge (5)
Ruishton Primary Academy, Ruishton

Sylvie's First Riddle

What could it be?
Follow the clues and see.

It looks like **foam**.
It sounds like **a car horn**.
It smells like **pond water**.
It feels like **silk**.
It tastes **sweet**.

Have you guessed what it could be?
Look below and you will see,
It is...

Answer: A duck.

Sylvie Hopkins (5)
Ruishton Primary Academy, Ruishton

My First Riddle - The South West

Jacob's First Riddle

What could they be?
Follow the clues and see.

They look like **shells**.
They sound **crunchy**.
They smell **yummy**.
They feel **a little rough**.
They taste like **prawns**.

Have you guessed what they could be?
Look below and you will see,
They are...

Answer: Skips.

Jacob May (5)
Ruishton Primary Academy, Ruishton

James' First Riddle

What could it be?
Follow the clues and see.

It looks **shiny**.
It sounds **splashy**.
It smells **stinky**.
It feels **slippery**.
It tastes **yummy**.

Have you guessed what it could be?
Look below and you will see,
It is...

Answer: A fish.

James Joyce (5)
Ruishton Primary Academy, Ruishton

Georgie's First Riddle

What could it be?
Follow the clues and see.

It looks **yummy**.
It sounds **crunchy**.
It smells **nice**.
It feels **bumpy**.
It tastes **sweet**.

Have you guessed what it could be?
Look below and you will see,
It is...

Answer: A cookie.

Georgie Scribbins (5)
Ruishton Primary Academy, Ruishton

Lois' First Riddle

What could it be?
Follow the clues and see.

It looks **cute**.
It sounds like ***oink, oink***!
It smells **yucky**.
It feels **soft**.

Have you guessed what it could be?
Look below and you will see,
It is...

Answer: A pig.

Lois Scribbins (5)
Ruishton Primary Academy, Ruishton

Niall's First Riddle

What could they be?
Follow the clues and see.

They look **yellow and flat with a pink packet**.
They sound **crunchy and they snap**.
They smell like **a prawn cocktail**.
They feel **hard**.
They taste like **prawns**.

Have you guessed what they could be?
Look below and you will see,
They are...

Answer: Prawn cocktail crisps.

Niall Hackett (5)
St Michael's CE Primary School, Stoke Gifford

Kian's First Riddle

What could they be?
Follow the clues and see.

They look **comfy**.
They sound like **Daddy's footsteps**.
They smell **cheesy and stinky**.
They feel **soft, cosy and sweaty**.
They taste like **yucky toes**.

Have you guessed what they could be?
Look below and you will see,
They are…

Answer: Dad's slippers.

Kian McMillan (5)
St Michael's CE Primary School, Stoke Gifford

Omisha's First Riddle

What could it be?
Follow the clues and see.

It looks like **different shapes**.
It sounds **squeaky and goes** *bang!*
It smells **rubbery**.
It feels **smooth and squidgy**.
It tastes **airy and yucky**.

Have you guessed what it could be?
Look below and you will see,
It is...

Answer: A balloon.

Omisha Gulla (5)
St Michael's CE Primary School, Stoke Gifford

Nicole's First Riddle

What could it be?
Follow the clues and see.

It looks like **a grape with a horn**.
It sounds like *neigh*!
It smells like **a strawberry**.
It feels **fluffy**.
It tastes like **cake**.

Have you guessed what it could be?
Look below and you will see,
It is...

Answer: A unicorn.

Nicole Celma (4)
St Michael's CE Primary School, Stoke Gifford

Vihaan's First Riddle

What could it be?
Follow the clues and see.

It looks **black and white**.
It sounds **crunchy**.
It smells like **a treat**.
It feels **round and hard**.
It tastes **yummy and creamy**.

Have you guessed what it could be?
Look below and you will see,
It is...

Answer: An Oreo biscuit.

Vihaan Arun (4)
St Michael's CE Primary School, Stoke Gifford

Nicol's First Riddle

What could it be?
Follow the clues and see.

It looks **white and oval**.
It sounds **crunchy**.
It smells **fantastic**.
It feels **cold and sweet**.
It tastes **sweet and delicious**.

Have you guessed what it could be?
Look below and you will see,
It is...

Answer: Ice cream.

Nicol Abbas (5)
St Michael's CE Primary School, Stoke Gifford

Hannah's First Riddle

What could it be?
Follow the clues and see.

It looks like **red and brown triangles**.
It sounds **crunchy**.
It smells **delicious**.
It feels **sticky**.
It tastes **great**.

Have you guessed what it could be?
Look below and you will see,
It is...

Answer: Jam on toast.

Hannah Downie (5)
St Michael's CE Primary School, Stoke Gifford

Jessica's First Riddle

What could it be?
Follow the clues and see.

It looks **feathery**.
It sounds **sploshy**.
It smells **wet**.
It feels like **it's going to flap**.
It **is too fast to catch**.

Have you guessed what it could be?
Look below and you will see,
It is...

Answer: A duck.

Jessica Lewis (5)
St Michael's CE Primary School, Stoke Gifford

Rohan's First Riddle

What could it be?
Follow the clues and see.

It looks **oval in shape**.
It sounds **crunchy**.
It smells **yummy**.
It feels **smooth**.
It tastes **very sweet**.

Have you guessed what it could be?
Look below and you will see,
It is...

Answer: A chocolate egg.

Rohan Mehta (5)
St Michael's CE Primary School, Stoke Gifford

Aila's First Riddle

What could it be?
Follow the clues and see.

It looks **green**.
It sounds **snappy**.
It smells **stinky**.
It feels **bumpy**.
It tastes **disgusting**.

Have you guessed what it could be?
Look below and you will see,
It is...

Answer: A crocodile.

Aila Geddes (5)
St Michael's CE Primary School, Stoke Gifford

Connor's First Riddle

What could it be?
Follow the clues and see.

It looks **brown**.
It sounds **quiet**.
It smells **sweet**.
It feels **smooth**.
It tastes **yummy**.

Have you guessed what it could be?
Look below and you will see,
It is...

Answer: Chocolate.

Connor Wotton (4)
St Michael's CE Primary School, Stoke Gifford

Lyla's First Riddle

What could it be?
Follow the clues and see.

It looks **red and juicy**.
It smells like **summer**.
It feels **lumpy in jam**.
It tastes **yummy**.

Have you guessed what it could be?
Look below and you will see,
It is…

Answer: A strawberry.

Lyla Viney (4)
St Michael's CE Primary School, Stoke Gifford

Tom's First Riddle

What could it be?
Follow the clues and see.

It looks **yellow, long and slightly tilted.**
It **does not make a sound.**
It smells **fresh and sweet.**
It feels **wet inside, soft and it has a bit of hard skin.**
It tastes **sweet.**

Have you guessed what it could be?
Look below and you will see,
It is...

Answer: A banana.

Tom Sinoradzki (5)
St Paul's CE Primary School, Gloucester

Ricards' First Riddle

What could it be?
Follow the clues and see.

It looks like **a heart and it is red.**
It **makes no sound.**
It smells **sweet.**
It feels **juicy when you eat it.**
It tastes **delicious, sometimes sour and sweet.**

Have you guessed what it could be?
Look below and you will see,
It is...

Answer: A strawberry.

Ricards Savickis (4)
St Paul's CE Primary School, Gloucester

Calvin's First Riddle

What could it be?
Follow the clues and see.

It looks **lumpy**.
It sounds **poppy**.
It smells **delicious**.
It feels **bumpy**.
It tastes **sweet**.

Have you guessed what it could be?
Look below and you will see,
It is...

Answer: Popcorn.

Calvin Omari Francis (4)
St Paul's CE Primary School, Gloucester

Esther's First Riddle

What could it be?
Follow the clues and see.

It looks **puffy and the shape of a cloud**.
It sounds like *snap, crackle, pop* **when heated**.
It smells **salty, sweet and buttery**.
It feels **squishy, crunchy and light**.
It tastes **sweet and savoury and delicious to eat**.

Have you guessed what it could be?
Look below and you will see,
It is...

Answer: Popcorn.

Esther Bennett (4)
Stalbridge CE Primary School, Stalbridge

Leo's First Riddle

What could it be?
Follow the clues and see.

It looks **with its eyes**.
It sounds **with its mouth**.
It smells **with its nose**.
It feels **with its hands**.
It tastes **with its tongue**.

Have you guessed what it could be?
Look below and you will see,
It is...

Answer: A human.

Leo Fortino (4)
Stalbridge CE Primary School, Stalbridge

Oliver's First Riddle

What could it be?
Follow the clues and see.

It looks **pink with a curly tail**.
It **grunts and squeals**.
It smells **of mud**.
It feels **soft**.
It tastes **yummy in my tummy**.

Have you guessed what it could be?
Look below and you will see,
It is...

Answer: A pig.

Oliver Newberry (5)
Stalbridge CE Primary School, Stalbridge

Aurelia's First Riddle

What could it be?
Follow the clues and see.

It looks **blue**.
It sounds like ***whoosh!***
It smells like **fish**.
It feels **cold**.
It tastes **salty**.

Have you guessed what it could be?
Look below and you will see,
It is...

Answer: *The sea.*

Aurelia Lux Turner (5)
Stalbridge CE Primary School, Stalbridge

Edward's First Riddle

What could it be?
Follow the clues and see.

It looks like **a worm**.
It sounds **sizzly**.
It smells **tasty**.
It feels **squidgy**.
It tastes **delicious**.

Have you guessed what it could be?
Look below and you will see,
It is...

Answer: A sausage.

Edward Mitchell (5)
Stalbridge CE Primary School, Stalbridge

Harry's First Riddle

What could it be?
Follow the clues and see.

It looks **purple**.
It sounds like **water**.
It smells **sweet**.
It feels **wet**.
It tastes **like blackcurrant**.

Have you guessed what it could be?
Look below and you will see,
It is...

Answer: Ribena.

Harry Stickland (5)
Stalbridge CE Primary School, Stalbridge

Nathan's First Riddle

What could it be?
Follow the clues and see.

It looks **nice**.
It sounds **squishy**.
It smells **yummy**.
It feels **fluffy**.
It tastes **sweet**.

Have you guessed what it could be?
Look below and you will see,
It is...

Answer: A marshmallow.

Nathan Collins (5)
Stalbridge CE Primary School, Stalbridge

Marley's First Riddle

What could it be?
Follow the clues and see.

It looks **slimy**.
It sounds **strange**.
It smells like **a pond**.
It feels **wet**.
It tastes **yucky**.

Have you guessed what it could be?
Look below and you will see,
It is...

Answer: A frog.

Marley Beau Cooper (5)
Stalbridge CE Primary School, Stalbridge

Tabitha's First Riddle

This is my riddle about a fantastic person. Who could it be? Follow the clues to see!

This person has **lovely, long, brown** hair,
Peppa Pig clothes are what they like to wear.
They like to watch **'Peppa Pig' and 'Mr Bean'** on TV,
And play **dollies** with me.
They like **pizza and ice cream** to eat,
And sometimes **chocolate** for a treat.
Peppa Pig World is their favourite thing,
And **nursery rhymes** are what they sing.
Albie is their best friend,
And now this riddle is at the end.

Have you guessed who it could be?
Look below and you will see, it is...

Answer: *Martha Grace.*

Tabitha Emily Williams (5)
Treleigh Community Primary School, Treleigh

My First Riddle - The South West

Dottie's First Riddle

This is my riddle about a fantastic person.
Who could it be? Follow the clues to see!

This person has **short, brown** hair,
A car jumper is what they like to wear.
They like to watch **'Top Wings'** on TV,
And play **Numberjacks** with me.
They like **sausage and mash** to eat,
And sometimes **chocolate** for a treat.
Going to the park is their favourite thing,
And **'A Million Dreams'** is what they sing.
Dottie is their best friend,
And now this riddle is at the end.

Have you guessed who it could be?
Look below and you will see, it is...

Answer: Eric.

Dottie Ellen Valentine Till (5)
Treleigh Community Primary School, Treleigh

Aiden's First Riddle

This is my riddle about a fantastic person.
Who could it be? Follow the clues to see!

This person has **nice, long** hair,
Yellow dresses are what they like to wear.
They like to watch **robots** on TV,
And play **mums and dads** with me.
They like **bananas** to eat,
And sometimes **yummy sweets** for a treat.
Playing with their dog is their favourite thing,
And **'Legendary Lovers'** is what they sing.
Aiden, of course, is their best friend,
And now this riddle is at the end.

Have you guessed who it could be?
Look below and you will see, it is...

Answer: Katy.

Aiden Hill (5)
Treleigh Community Primary School, Treleigh

My First Riddle - The South West

Lottie's First Riddle

This is my riddle about a fantastic person. Who could it be? Follow the clues to see!

This person has **short, brown** hair,
A pretty dress is what they like to wear.
They like to watch **'Britain's Got Talent'** on TV,
And play **it** with me.
They like **spaghetti** to eat,
And sometimes **Haribo** for a treat.
Going outside is their favourite thing,
And **'Shotgun'** is what they sing.
Lottie is their best friend,
And now this riddle is at the end.

Have you guessed who it could be?
Look below and you will see, it is...

Answer: Mrs Williams.

Lottie Maybank (5)
Treleigh Community Primary School, Treleigh

Tiberius' First Riddle

This is my riddle about a fantastic person.
Who could it be? Follow the clues to see!

This person has **a long plait in their** hair,
A yellow dress is what they like to wear.
They like to watch **robots** on TV,
And play **mums and dads** with me.
They like **fish and chips** to eat,
And sometimes **chocolate** for a treat.
Their pet dog is their favourite thing,
And **'Legendary Lovers'** is what they sing.
Orla is their best friend,
And now this riddle is at the end.

Have you guessed who it could be?
Look below and you will see, it is...

Answer: Katie.

Tiberius Moore (5)
Treleigh Community Primary School, Treleigh

Emilia's First Riddle

This is my riddle about a fantastic person.
Who could it be? Follow the clues to see!

This person has **pretty, long** hair,
Nice T-shirts are what they like to wear.
They like to watch **robots** on TV,
And play **hide-and-seek** with me.
They like **hot dogs** to eat,
And sometimes **chocolate** for a treat.
Playing with the dog is their favourite thing,
And **'Legendary Lovers'** is what they sing.
Orla is their best friend,
And now this riddle is at the end.

Have you guessed who it could be?
Look below and you will see, it is...

Answer: Caty.

Emilia Woodard (4)
Treleigh Community Primary School, Treleigh

Abbie's First Riddle

This is my riddle about a fantastic person. Who could it be? Follow the clues to see!

This person has **black** hair,
Yellow stuff is what they like to wear.
They like to watch **'Peppa Pig'** on TV,
And play **mums and dads** with me.
They like **chicken noodles** to eat,
And sometimes **sweets** for a treat.
Playing is their favourite thing,
And **'Jingle Bells'** is what they sing.
Abbie is their best friend,
And now this riddle is at the end.

Have you guessed who it could be?
Look below and you will see, it is...

Answer: Chloe.

Abbie Williams
Treleigh Community Primary School, Treleigh

Orla's First Riddle

This is my riddle about a fantastic person. Who could it be? Follow the clues to see!

This person has **brown** hair,
A pink and purple dress is what they like to wear.
They like to watch **'Sunny Bunnies'** on TV,
And play **catch** with me.
They like **fish and chips** to eat,
And sometimes **sweets** for a treat.
Playing is their favourite thing,
And **the weather song** is what they sing.
Orla is their best friend,
And now this riddle is at the end.

Have you guessed who it could be?
Look below and you will see, it is...

Answer: Katie.

Orla Bray (5)
Treleigh Community Primary School, Treleigh

Thomas' First Riddle

This is my riddle about a fantastic person.
Who could it be? Follow the clues to see!

This person has **long, brown** hair,
A bunny top is what they like to wear.
They like to watch **'Peppa Pig'** on TV,
And play **Simon Says** with me.
They like **sandwiches** to eat,
And sometimes **sweets** for a treat.
Mushrooms are their favourite thing,
And **'Go Jetters'** is what they sing.
Poppy is their best friend,
And now this riddle is at the end.

Have you guessed who it could be?
Look below and you will see, it is...

Answer: Emelia.

Thomas Peerless (5)
Treleigh Community Primary School, Treleigh

Dylan's First Riddle

This is my riddle about a fantastic person. Who could it be? Follow the clues to see!

This person has **white, short** hair,
Jumpers are what they like to wear.
They like to watch **the news** on TV,
And play **fun Lego** with me.
They like **yummy pizza** to eat,
And sometimes **chocolate** for a treat.
Minecraft is their favourite thing,
And **'Everything Is Awesome'** is what they sing.
Oscar is their best friend,
And now this riddle is at the end.

Have you guessed who it could be?
Look below and you will see, it is...

Answer: Harry.

Dylan Merrett-Cope (4)
Treleigh Community Primary School, Treleigh

Ezmae's First Riddle

This is my riddle about a fantastic person.
Who could it be? Follow the clues to see!

This person has **brown** hair,
Sparkles are what they like to wear.
They like to watch **'Peppa Pig'** on TV,
And play **houses** with me.
They like **burgers** to eat,
And sometimes **cupcakes** for a treat.
Playing is their favourite thing,
And **'Let It Go'** is what they sing.
Ezmae is their best friend,
And now this riddle is at the end.

Have you guessed who it could be?
Look below and you will see, it is...

Answer: Emily S.

Ezmae Cooke (5)
Treleigh Community Primary School, Treleigh

Jowan's First Riddle

This is my riddle about a fantastic person.
Who could it be? Follow the clues to see!

This person has **brown, long** hair,
Dresses are what they like to wear.
They like to watch a **film** on TV,
And play **Simon Says** with me.
They like **spicy pizza** to eat,
And sometimes **popcorn** for a treat.
Holidays are their favourite thing,
And **a happy song** is what they sing.
Jenson is their best friend,
And now this riddle is at the end.

Have you guessed who it could be?
Look below and you will see, it is...

Answer: Miss Daniels.

Jowan Kershaw (4)
Treleigh Community Primary School, Treleigh

Sapphire's First Riddle

This is my riddle about a fantastic person.
Who could it be? Follow the clues to see!

This person has **yellow** hair,
A cap is what they like to wear.
They like to watch **the news** on TV,
And play **hide-and-seek** with me.
They like **a jacket potato** to eat,
And sometimes **sweets** for a treat.
Playing is their favourite thing,
And **'Agadoo'** is what they sing.
Oscar is their best friend,
And now this riddle is at the end.

Have you guessed who it could be?
Look below and you will see, it is...

Answer: Harry.

Sapphire Mitchell (5)
Treleigh Community Primary School, Treleigh

Erin's First Riddle

This is my riddle about a fantastic person. Who could it be? Follow the clues to see!

This person has **plaits** in her hair,
A L.O.L top is what they like to wear.
They like to watch **films** on TV,
And play **tag** with me.
They like **pizza** to eat,
And sometimes **chocolate** for a treat.
Playing outside is their favourite thing,
And **the alphabet** is what they sing.
Erin is their best friend,
And now this riddle is at the end.

Have you guessed who it could be?
Look below and you will see, it is...

Answer: *Emily K.*

Erin Millard (5)
Treleigh Community Primary School, Treleigh

Lewis' First Riddle

This is my riddle about a fantastic person. Who could it be? Follow the clues to see!

This person has **brown, curly** hair,
Rainbows are what they like to wear.
They like to watch **CBeebies** on TV,
And play **chase** with me.
They like **sausages** to eat,
And sometimes **sweets** for a treat.
Playing is their favourite thing,
And **a nice song** is what they sing.
Lewis is their best friend,
And now this riddle is at the end.

Have you guessed who it could be?
Look below and you will see, it is...

Answer: Molly.

Lewis Pooley (5)
Treleigh Community Primary School, Treleigh

Max's First Riddle

What could it be?
Follow the clues and see.

It looks like **it's hanging**.
It sounds like *bump, bump!*
It smells like **popcorn**.
It feels like **a steering wheel**.
It tastes like **popcorn**.

Have you guessed what it could be?
Look below and you will see,
It is...

Answer: A bumper car.

Max Sims (4)
Trewirgie Infants' School, Redruth

Laura's First Riddle

Who could they be?
Follow the clues and see.

They look like **a princess**.
They sound like **your favourite song**.
They smell like **flowers**.
They feel **nice and soft**.
They taste like **red fruit**.

Have you guessed who it could be?
Look below and you will see,
They are...

Answer: Elsa.

Laura Stukaite (5)
Trewirgie Infants' School, Redruth

Clara's First Riddle

What could it be?
Follow the clues and see.

It looks **fun**.
It sounds like **a merry-go-round**.
It smells like **popcorn and lollipops**.
It feels **hard**.
It tastes like **candyfloss**.

Have you guessed what it could be?
Look below and you will see,
It is...

Answer: The funfair.

Clara Davies (5)
Trewirgie Infants' School, Redruth

Ollie's First Riddle

Who could it be?
Follow the clues and see.

They look **blue and red**.
They sound like ***bang, bang, jump!***
They smell like **bogeys**.
They feel **crunchy**.
They taste **bony**.

Have you guessed who it could be?
Look below and you will see,
It is...

Answer: *Spider-Man.*

Ollie Jack Hutchens (5)
Trewirgie Infants' School, Redruth

Olivia's First Riddle

What could it be?
Follow the clues and see.

It looks like **a scaly, shiny tail**.
It sounds **squishy**.
It smells like **seaweed**.
It feels **soft and scaly**.
It tastes like **fish**.

Have you guessed what it could be?
Look below and you will see,
It is...

Answer: A mermaid.

Olivia Cooper (5)
Trewirgie Infants' School, Redruth

Our First Riddle

What could it be?
Follow the clues and see.

It looks like **a shiny, pink tail**.
It sounds like **splashing**.
It smells like **the salty sea**.
It feels **wet**.
It tastes **salty**.

Have you guessed what it could be?
Look below and you will see,
It is...

Answer: A mermaid.

Phoenix (5) & Alanna
Trewirgie Infants' School, Redruth

Noah's First Riddle

What could it be?
Follow the clues and see.

It looks like **a fish's tail**.
It sounds **splashy**.
It smells like **flowers**.
It feels **scaly**.
It tastes **bony, yuck!**

Have you guessed what it could be?
Look below and you will see,
It is...

Answer: A mermaid.

Noah Jones (5)
Trewirgie Infants' School, Redruth

Violet's First Riddle

Who could it be?
Follow the clues and see.

They look like **a hero**.
They sound like **webbing**.
They smell like **grass**.
They feel **soft**.
They taste like **webs**.

Have you guessed who it could be?
Look below and you will see,
It is...

Answer: *Spider-Gwen.*

Violet Mckenzie (5)
Trewirgie Infants' School, Redruth

Alia's First Riddle

What could it be?
Follow the clues and see.

It looks **pink**.
It sounds like **a window**.
It smells like **air freshener**.
It feels like **metal**.
It tastes like **metal**.

Have you guessed what it could be?
Look below and you will see,
It is...

Answer: A car.

Alia Marie Blaber (4)
Trewirgie Infants' School, Redruth

Alfie's First Riddle

What could it be?
Follow the clues and see.

It looks **blue and yellow**.
It sounds **windy**.
It smells of **ice cream**.
It feels **soggy**.
It tastes **salty**.

Have you guessed what it could be?
Look below and you will see,
It is...

Answer: *The beach.*

Alfie Thomas Hart (4)
Trewirgie Infants' School, Redruth

Amelia's First Riddle

What could it be?
Follow the clues and see.

It looks **colourful**.
It sounds **crunchy**.
It smells **sweet**.
It feels **sticky**.
It tastes **yummy**.

Have you guessed what it could be?
Look below and you will see,
It is...

Answer: A rainbow Skittle.

Amelia Natasha Hunter (5)
Trewirgie Infants' School, Redruth

Harvey's First Riddle

What could it be?
Follow the clues and see.

It looks **fun**.
It sounds **loud**.
It smells like **a lolly**.
It feels **hard**.
It tastes like **ice cream**.

Have you guessed what it could be?
Look below and you will see,
It is...

Answer: *The funfair.*

Harvey Imchichi (5)
Trewirgie Infants' School, Redruth

My First Riddle - The South West

Jessica's First Riddle

What could it be?
Follow the clues and see.

It looks **fun**.
It sounds **loud**.
It smells like **flowers**.
It feels **nice**.
It tastes like **a picnic**.

Have you guessed what it could be?
Look below and you will see,
It is...

Answer: *The park.*

Jessica Lowndes (5)
Trewirgie Infants' School, Redruth

Cody's First Riddle

What could it be?
Follow the clues and see.

It looks **blue**.
It sounds like **an engine**.
It smells like **tyres**.
It feels **smooth**.
It tastes **smoky**.

Have you guessed what it could be?
Look below and you will see,
It is...

Answer: A car.

Cody Holloway (5)
Trewirgie Infants' School, Redruth

Sophie's First Riddle

What could it be?
Follow the clues and see.

It looks **swirly**.
It sounds **crunchy**.
It smells like **candy**.
It feels **sticky**.
It tastes **yummy**.

Have you guessed what it could be?
Look below and you will see,
It is...

Answer: A lollipop.

Sophie Miller (5)
Trewirgie Infants' School, Redruth

Isla's First Riddle

What could it be?
Follow the clues and see.

It looks **yummy**.
It sounds **crunchy**.
It smells like **candy**.
It feels **cold**.
It tastes **yummy**.

Have you guessed what it could be?
Look below and you will see,
It is...

Answer: An ice lolly.

Isla Clarke (5)
Trewirgie Infants' School, Redruth

Harlan's First Riddle

What could it be?
Follow the clues and see.

It looks like **a circle**.
It sounds **crunchy**.
It smells **sweet**.
It feels **hard**.
It tastes **juicy**.

Have you guessed what it could be?
Look below and you will see,
It is...

Answer: An apple.

Harlan Massey (5)
Trewirgie Infants' School, Redruth

Alex's First Riddle

What could it be?
Follow the clues and see.

It looks **red**.
It sounds **loud**.
It smells like **dust**.
It feels **hard**.
It tastes like **electricity**.

Have you guessed what it could be?
Look below and you will see,
It is...

Answer: A jet.

Alex Guppy-Wilcox (5)
Trewirgie Infants' School, Redruth

James' First Riddle

What could it be?
Follow the clues and see.

It looks like **a ball**.
It sounds **crunchy**.
It smells **nice**.
It feels **soft**.
It tastes **sweet**.

Have you guessed what it could be?
Look below and you will see,
It is...

Answer: A lollipop.

James Pullin (5)
Trewirgie Infants' School, Redruth

Mason's First Riddle

What could it be?
Follow the clues and see.

It looks **delicious**.
It sounds **squelchy**.
It smells **yummy**.
It feels **cold**.
It tastes **tasty**.

Have you guessed what it could be?
Look below and you will see,
It is...

Answer: Ice cream.

Mason Summers (5)
Trewirgie Infants' School, Redruth

My First Riddle - The South West

Isla's First Riddle

What could it be?
Follow the clues and see.

It looks **round**.
It sounds **squeaky**.
It smells **muddy**.
It feels **bouncy**.
It tastes **muddy**.

Have you guessed what it could be?
Look below and you will see,
It is...

Answer: A football.

Isla Roberts (5)
Trewirgie Infants' School, Redruth

Millie's First Riddle

What could it be?
Follow the clues and see.

It looks **pink**.
It sounds **crunchy**.
It smells **yummy**.
It feels **wet**.
It tastes **nice**.

Have you guessed what it could be?
Look below and you will see,
It is...

Answer: A pink lollipop.

Millie Smith (4)
Trewirgie Infants' School, Redruth

Our First Riddle

What could it be?
Follow the clues and see.

It looks **yummy**.
It sounds **crunchy**.
It smells **sweet**.
It feels **cold**.
It tastes **delicious**.

Have you guessed what it could be?
Look below and you will see,
It is...

Answer: A lolly.

Lando Winchester (5), Lennon, Gabriella Wooten, Harley, Lily-Lea (5), Elsa Victoria-Louise Hill & Kennedy Mila Allison
Trewirgie Infants' School, Redruth

Laith's First Riddle

What could it be?
Follow the clues and see.

It looks like **a boat**.
It sounds **quiet**.
It smells **sweet**.
It feels **soft**.
It tastes **nice**.

Have you guessed what it could be?
Look below and you will see,
It is...

Answer: A banana.

Laith Wills (4)
Trewirgie Infants' School, Redruth

Our First Riddle

What could it be?
Follow the clues and see.

It looks **dark**.
It sounds **crunchy**.
It smells **tasty**.
It feels **smooth**.
It tastes **yummy**.

Have you guessed what it could be?
Look below and you will see,
It is...

Answer: Chocolate.

Summer Crocker (4), Ethan, Laylah & Archie Jacka
Trewirgie Infants' School, Redruth

Florie's First Riddle

What could it be?
Follow the clues and see.

It looks **oval**.
It sounds **crunchy**.
It smells **nice**.
It feels **hot**.
It tastes **really nice**.

Have you guessed what it could be?
Look below and you will see,
It is...

Answer: A fish.

Florie Creeden (4)
Trewirgie Infants' School, Redruth

Lola's First Riddle

What could it be?
Follow the clues and see.

It looks **pink**.
It sounds **noisy**.
It smells **sweet**.
It feels **sticky**.
It tastes **sweet**.

Have you guessed what it could be?
Look below and you will see,
It is...

Answer: A lollipop.

Lola Curnow (5)
Trewirgie Infants' School, Redruth

Luke's First Riddle

What could it be?
Follow the clues and see.

It looks **brown**.
It sounds **crunchy**.
It smells **sweet**.
It feels **hard**.
It tastes **yummy**.

Have you guessed what it could be?
Look below and you will see,
It is...

Answer: Chocolate.

Luke Matthews (5)
Trewirgie Infants' School, Redruth

Alanna's First Riddle

What could it be?
Follow the clues and see.

It looks **round**.
It sounds **crunchy**.
It smells **sweet**.
It feels **wet**.
It tastes **juicy**.

Have you guessed what it could be?
Look below and you will see,
It is...

Answer: An apple.

Alanna Freya Isaacs (5)
Trewirgie Infants' School, Redruth

Elian's First Riddle

What could it be?
Follow the clues and see.

It looks **bendy**.
It sounds **quiet**.
It smells **yummy**.
It feels **soft**.
It tastes **nice**.

Have you guessed what it could be?
Look below and you will see,
It is...

Answer: A banana.

Elian Thomas (4)
Trewirgie Infants' School, Redruth

Arya's First Riddle

What could it be?
Follow the clues and see.

It looks **big**.
It sounds **slurpy**.
It smells **nice**.
It feels **cold**.
It tastes **yummy**.

Have you guessed what it could be?
Look below and you will see,
It is...

Answer: Ice cream.

Arya Spry (5)
Trewirgie Infants' School, Redruth

Cohen's First Riddle

What could it be?
Follow the clues and see.

It looks **red**.
It sounds **fast**.
It smells **fresh**.
It feels **soft**.
It tastes **smoky**.

Have you guessed what it could be?
Look below and you will see,
It is...

Answer: A car.

Cohen Taylor (5)
Trewirgie Infants' School, Redruth

Mollie's First Riddle

What could it be?
Follow the clues and see.

It looks **big**.
It sounds **quiet**.
It smells **yummy**.
It feels **hot**.
It tastes **soft**.

Have you guessed what it could be?
Look below and you will see,
It is...

Answer: A bun.

Mollie Jonik (5)
Trewirgie Infants' School, Redruth

Dylan's First Riddle

What could it be?
Follow the clues and see.

It looks **round**.
It sounds **quiet**.
It smells **fruity**.
It feels **squishy**.
It tastes **scrumptious**.

Have you guessed what it could be?
Look below and you will see,
It is...

Answer: An orange.

Dylan Finley Robert King (5)
Wareham St Mary Primary School, Wareham

My First Riddle - The South West

Harlie's First Riddle

What could it be?
Follow the clues and see.

It looks **yellow**.
It sounds **quiet**.
It smells **fruity**.
It feels **smooth**.
It tastes **delicious**.

Have you guessed what it could be?
Look below and you will see,
It is...

Answer: A banana.

Harlie Fenton (5)
Wareham St Mary Primary School, Wareham

Emilija's First Riddle

What could it be?
Follow the clues and see.

It looks **bumpy**.
It sounds **crunchy**.
It smells **yummy**.
It feels **spiky**.
It tastes **sour**.

Have you guessed what it could be?
Look below and you will see,
It is...

Answer: A pineapple.

Emilija Hughes (4)
Wareham St Mary Primary School, Wareham

My First Riddle - The South West

Keira-Leigh's First Riddle

What could it be?
Follow the clues and see.

It looks **so big**.
It sounds **squidgy**.
It smells **yummy**.
It feels **bumpy**.
It tastes **juicy**.

Have you guessed what it could be?
Look below and you will see,
It is...

Answer: An orange.

Keira-Leigh Baynton (5)
Wareham St Mary Primary School, Wareham

Rory's First Riddle

What could it be?
Follow the clues and see.

It looks **round**.
It sounds **crunchy**.
It smells **sweet**.
It feels **squishy**.
It tastes **yummy**.

Have you guessed what it could be?
Look below and you will see,
It is...

Answer: A grape.

Rory McConnell (5)
Wareham St Mary Primary School, Wareham

Zachary's First Riddle

What could it be?
Follow the clues and see.

It looks **purple**.
It sounds **squeaky**.
It smells **sweet**.
It feels **smooth**.
It tastes **sugary**.

Have you guessed what it could be?
Look below and you will see,
It is...

Answer: A plum.

Zachary Lee Knowles (5)
Wareham St Mary Primary School, Wareham

Molly's First Riddle

What could it be?
Follow the clues and see.

It looks **purple**.
It sounds **quiet**.
It smells **sweet**.
It feels **squishy**.
It tastes **juicy**.

Have you guessed what it could be?
Look below and you will see,
It is...

Answer: A grape.

Molly Lee (5)
Wareham St Mary Primary School, Wareham

Alexandra's First Riddle

What could it be?
Follow the clues and see.

It looks **yellow**.
It sounds **quiet**.
It smells **fresh**.
It feels **soft**.
It tastes **fruity**.

Have you guessed what it could be?
Look below and you will see,
It is...

Answer: A banana.

Alexandra Pitman (5)
Wareham St Mary Primary School, Wareham

Peter's First Riddle

What could it be?
Follow the clues and see.

It looks **purple**.
It sounds **loud**.
It smells **fresh**.
It feels **smooth**.
It tastes **juicy**.

Have you guessed what it could be?
Look below and you will see,
It is...

Answer: A grape.

Peter John Nurdin (5)
Wareham St Mary Primary School, Wareham

Sienna's First Riddle

What could it be?
Follow the clues and see.

It looks **round**.
It sounds **quiet**.
It smells **fresh**.
It feels **smooth**.
It tastes **juicy**.

Have you guessed what it could be?
Look below and you will see,
It is...

Answer: A grape.

Sienna Helen Wells (5)
Wareham St Mary Primary School, Wareham

Emily's First Riddle

What could it be?
Follow the clues and see.

It looks **green**.
It sounds **calm**.
It smells **fruity**.
It feels **squishy**.
It tastes **sour**.

Have you guessed what it could be?
Look below and you will see,
It is...

Answer: A lime.

Emily Chrissy Williams (5)
Wareham St Mary Primary School, Wareham

Jacob's First Riddle

What could it be?
Follow the clues and see.

It looks **purple**.
It sounds **quiet**.
It smells **fresh**.
It feels **cold**.
It tastes **yummy**.

Have you guessed what it could be?
Look below and you will see,
It is...

Answer: A grape.

Jacob Hobbs-Smith (5)
Wareham St Mary Primary School, Wareham

YoungWriters® Est. 1991

YOUNG WRITERS INFORMATION

We hope you have enjoyed reading this book – and that you will continue to in the coming years.

If you're a young writer who enjoys reading and creative writing, or the parent of an enthusiastic poet or story writer, do visit our website **www.youngwriters.co.uk**. Here you will find free competitions, workshops and games, as well as recommended reads, a poetry glossary and our blog. There's lots to keep budding writers motivated to write!

If you would like to order further copies of this book, or any of our other titles, then please give us a call or order via your online account.

Young Writers
Remus House
Coltsfoot Drive
Peterborough
PE2 9BF
(01733) 890066
info@youngwriters.co.uk

Join in the conversation!
Tips, news, giveaways and much more!

f YoungWritersUK   **@YoungWritersCW**